The

BREAKFAST TACO

Book

SECOND EDITION

by Hilah Johnson

THE BREAKFAST TACO BOOK
SECOND EDITION
by Hilah Johnson

Photos by Hilah Johnson and Christopher Sharpe

ISBN: 978-0-9886736-2-5
Second Edition: December 2013
First Edition: June 2010

OTHER BOOKS BY HILAH JOHNSON
Learn to Cook

Cavelady Cooking

Holiday Cookies

CONTENTS

PART ONE:
ALL HAIL BREAKFAST TACOS

7   Introduction to Breakfast Tacos

19   Breakfast Taco History

27   My Breakfast Taco Tour

PART TWO:
HOW TO MAKE BREAKFAST TACOS

34   Tortillas

39   Salsa

44   **Taco Guts: The Classics**

46   Scrambled Eggs

       Beans

       Home Fries

       Bacon

       Homemade Chorizo

       Nopalitos

       Hangover Tacos

57   **Tacos Especiales**

       The Carter

       Migas

       Green Eggs and Ham

       Sweet Potato and Black Bean

       The Lou-chadore

       The Heath

70   Thanks for Reading

PART ONE

ALL HAIL BREAKFAST TACOS!

BREAKFAST TACO BASICS

Breakfast tacos in plain, unmarked bag.

Piping-hot breakfast tacos wrapped in foil.

Add salsa and enjoy.

INTRODUCTION

Growing up in Austin, I have eaten more than my fair share of breakfast tacos over the course of my life.

If you're from Texas, you know what I mean. If you're not, then what I mean is that I cut my teeth on breakfast tacos, and when I'm old and gray I'll probably be cutting my gums on them, too. Indeed, if you're not from Texas, you might not even know what the hell a breakfast taco is. That is why

I decided to write this compendium of breakfast taco history, lore, interviews, opinions, facts, stuff I made up, and recipes.

In this second edition of *The Breakfast Taco Book,* I actually did some research -- *gasp!* -- on the origination of the breakfast taco. But don't expect any solid answers. Like most popular and widely spread foods, the exact place and date of conception of the breakfast taco is impossible to know. There are some undeniable truths and some expert opinions, however, and I'll share them with you. In this edition, I explored outside Austin to San Antonio, and even farther south to Seguin and Brownsville. Through scouring newspaper archives from the 1920s onward, I'm certain the breakfast taco as we know it today was first created in one of those four towns sometime in the early 1970s, and very likely independently stumbled upon by multiple cooks.

One thing I'm most excited about with this edition is the expanded recipe section. Ever heard of the "Jimmy Carter"? Invented in San Antonio in 1976, this breakfast taco made national news at the time. I've recreated it here for you. Also included are some tacos I made up: the Green Eggs and Ham; The Lou-Chadore, a Mexi-meat paradise; and a new high-protein vegan option.

Thank you for your purchase of this book. Your support helps our small business grow! In return, I hope my book gives you knowledge, laughs, and most importantly, delicious food.

¡Buen Provecho!

Hilah

WHAT THE HELL IS A BREAKFAST TACO?

This is a legitimate question, one that comes up often, and I can't fault you for asking. You'd think – or at least, I thought – that breakfast tacos were understood unanimously across this great big state.

Turns out, though, that even within Texas, there is some confusion. In fact, in some parts the names "breakfast burrito" and "breakfast taco" are used interchangeably. Say WHAT?!

Breakfast burritos in TEXAS? It's disappointingly true.

I spoke with Garrett Heath of the the popular San Antonio food blog, *SA Flavor*. Having grown up in Lubbock before moseying on to Old San Antone in 2005, Heath explains:

"Regardless of the size of the tortilla in the Texas Panhandle, it is always called a breakfast burrito; a taco is by default a crunchy shell. This caused a lot of confusion when I moved down to San Antonio and co-workers kept asking if I'd like a "egg and potato breakfast taco." I thought to myself, "Why in the world would someone want to put eggs and potatoes in a crunchy shell?" After turning them down for several weeks, I finally realized that a breakfast taco indeed had a soft tortilla."

He's loved them ever since.

Addie Broyles, food editor for the Austin American Statesman, and native of Missouri confirms his story:

"I've always made the equivalent of breakfast tacos at home, even growing up in Missouri, but I didn't realize how special they were to Austin until I went to Dallas and was forced to eat a breakfast burrito that everyone insisted was no different than a breakfast taco."

Oh, Panhandle! Oh, Dallas! *Hangs hat in shame* I honestly thought that we Texans could all hold hands and two-step under the Great Breakfast Taco Umbrella, but on the bright side this bolsters my argument that breakfast tacos are as special and unique to Central and South Texas as snow flakes, if we ever got any snow flakes around here.

Heath has a theory he calls the *I-20 Taco Theory* which states that north of highway I-20 you get burritos for breakfast and south of highway I-20 you get tacos. Highway I-20 cuts the state in half, from El Paso through to east Texas and into Shreveport, Louisiana. Heading westward on I-20 will take you all the way to Los Angeles.

This is where it gets interesting.

It's well established that the burrito (breakfast or otherwise) was made popular in the US by a restaurant called El Cholo Spanish Cafe located in Los Angeles in the 1930s. The theory is that burritos would have traveled from Los Angeles along major highways before settling into places like New Mexico, west Texas and the Texas Panhandle. I think by then, though, the Mexican influence of tacos on south and central Texas had too much of a stronghold for imported California burritos to overtake the region.

On restaurant menus from the Rio Grande Valley and up to Austin, breakfast tacos have a place of esteem. No Mexican or Tex-Mex joint, greasy spoon or diner would deign to not include breakfast tacos on their menus. Usually you'll get your choice of fillings—two or three—for one low price with the option to add additional fillings for an extra quarter or two a piece.

Fillings all over include the classic breakfast staples of scrambled eggs, pork sausage, bacon, ham, potatoes in some form (I've seen homefries, hashbrowns, and even mashed potatoes make their way into breakfast tacos) and cheese. The closer you move towards the border, it seems to me, the more options you get and breakfast taco menus may also embrace migas, rice, refried beans, nopales (cactus) and chorizo (pork sausage). Further still and you will be seduced by delicacies like weenie and egg tacos, machacado (Mexican chipped beef)

chicharrón (pork skin) and barbacoa (shredded beef). Salsa varieties vary, but both red and green are standard.

I want to be able to tell you with certainty exactly what constitutes a breakfast taco; what makes a breakfast taco different from any other taco. The fact is, in 2010 with the first edition of this book, I thought I knew. I really thought I had the answer. And these four requirements summed it up:

PORTABLE (they almost always come wrapped in foil for the guy or gal on the go)

MODEST (they are made with small tortillas and priced accordingly—cheap!)

EGGS (though there are some notable exceptions to this rule)

FLOUR TORTILLAS (. . . or not . . . more on this later)

I still stand by the first two requirements. Those are what separate a breakfast taco from a breakfast burrito. Those second two . . . well, I'm starting to question after exploring more about breakfast tacos not just in Austin, but all over Texas.

EGGS?

I spoke to my good friend Louis Fowler. Louis grew up in the tiny Texas town of Blooming Grove but now lives in Oklahoma, writing for the *Oklahoma Gazette* covering food and film. While Blooming Grove is located in the scalene triangle between Dallas, Waco, and Corsicana, Louis was fortunately blessed with a Mexican grandma who would visit from Brownsville and who introduced him to proper breakfast tacos made the way only a Mexican grandma can make them: with plenty of love and lard. When asked what defines a breakfast taco, he responded:

"I'd like to say eggs—take out the eggs and you might as well turn a breakfast taco into an anytime taco—but, really, isn't any taco served between 5 AM and 10:30 AM honestly a "breakfast" taco? Those are the official breakfast hours, right? But, then again, if you work the night shift, sleep during the day and eat breakfast at around 5 PM, that would be a...I mean you could...if...okay, let's just say eggs. Eggs."

Broyles said the same, but with more conviction:

"Breakfast tacos aren't really breakfast tacos without eggs, in my opinion. Some people might order just a potato and chorizo taco, but eggs really complete the taco."

I tend to agree with that, but there is more to the breakfast taco puzzle. I asked cookbook author, food historian, and eighth-generation Texan Melissa Guerra about her favorite breakfast taco fillings. Guerra grew up on a working cattle ranch in south Texas and now splits her time between there and San Antonio where she runs her cookware store, Melissa Guerra Latin Kitchen Market.

"My favorites are tacos de chicharrón en salsa verde (pork rinds in green sauce) but usually the work crews wipe them out before I get there. At home it's bean and cheese. However, the most powerful breakfast "taco" is a plain buttered flour tortilla. Turns both men and women into toddlers, nostalgic for the days when their grandmas would hand them a fresh one right off the comal. Such reveries, even a few tears."

Heath's favorites sound similar: "[My] standard order would be one bacon and egg and one bean and cheese. If it is a weekend, I am probably going for a barbacoa taco."

One night over micheladas on the back patio, with my mind firmly entrenched in this book, I asked my friend Carlos about "breakfast tacos" in Mexico. He's from Guadalajara and explained it like this: "In Mexico, we eat tacos for breakfast, but they're just like any other taco: barbacoa or something on a corn tortilla with onions, cilantro". So while "anytime" tacos can be eaten in the morning to break the fast, they're still not really "breakfast tacos", per se. Or are they?

Could it be that eggs and refried beans both count towards making an "anytime taco" into a "breakfast taco"? Could it also be that "anytime tacos" like barbacoa and chicharrón can turn into "breakfast tacos" simply by virtue of the time of day at which they are eaten? Could it be that a name ain't nothing but a word and maybe none of this even matters?! Oh, cruel world. I weep. Pass me a taco, please, and a Kleenex. And some more salsa, thanks.

You can see that defining a breakfast taco based solely on what is stuffed inside is tricky. In fact, perhaps part of the beauty of breakfast tacos and tacos generally is the thrifty idea that you could literally fill them with anything you happen to have. Yet I think most people would agree that while a taco without eggs can still be a breakfast taco, a taco with eggs will never be anything but a breakfast taco.

TORTILLAS?

My earliest memories of breakfast tacos involve a rushed weekday morning and my dad shoving a hot, foil-wrapped flour tortilla filled with eggs and potatoes into my backpack.

I'd eat it in back seat of the car on my way to school, leaving the balled up foil in the floor of my mom's car. To me, breakfast tacos are ALWAYS on flour tortillas. I was honestly very surprised to learn that while that's certainly the majority opinion as well, there are some dissidents who order breakfast tacos on corn tortillas regularly. Granted, these are the same people who eat barbacoa for breakfast, too. Down in their hearts, though, I think everyone knows that scrambled eggs and flour tortillas go together like a hand and glove.

Guerra has a funny reasoning behind it that fits:

"Flour tortillas are sweet and creamy, while corn have just a slightly bitter aftertaste. As for myself, my morning persona can be described as bitter. Giving me a flour breakfast taco in the morning improves everyone's day. Ask my kids."

I think she's onto something. Carlos Rivero, owner of *El Chilito* in Austin says there is something "decadent" about breakfast on a flour tortilla instead of corn. In Austin, especially, where the hangovers are a'plenty and the mornings can be rough around the edges, a flour tortilla soothes a whiskey-ravaged belly like no other tortilla can. Wash that down with a mimosa or a michelada and you're ready to rock and roll another day.

But here's what I think about all these in a nut shell.

(Or should I say taco shell? No, I shouldn't. Sorry!)

BREAKFAST TACOS:

These are from Texas and are difficult to find outside of Texas. Minimally stuffed, no bigger than a fist, and cheap. In fact, to find a breakfast taco with more than three different fillings inside is rare, and not recommended. Breakfast taco tortillas are generally less than 6 inches diameter, with the fillings scooped into the center and the tortilla rolled or folded over, leaving the ends open. Breakfast tacos to-go are always wrapped up in foil and tossed into a paper sack along with a handful of tiny salsa cups and (inexplicably) about a hundred salt packets. One of the best features of the breakfast taco is that they are small enough to fit in your hand, purse, pocket and mouth. Most people find that it takes two or three to make a meal, offering the opportunity to try a few different combinations. Variety is the spice of life AND of breakfast tacos.

BREAKFAST BURRITOS:

Found in California, New Mexico, and (evidently) northern regions of Texas. Large flour tortilla, stuffed tight with maximum fillings; transportable by pocket only if pockets in question are those of oversized clown pants. Breakfast burritos often have five or more fillings. Unless absolutely ravenous, you may find it difficult to finish an entire breakfast burrito. They can be as large as a Nerf football. The extra large tortilla is folded in

TACO TALK

Growing up, we were always going camping in Texas, New Mexico or Colorado. The breakfast of choice was always breakfast burritos, namely because you don't need a plate or utensils to eat it. In spite of the ashes that would always find a way into the skillet, a breakfast burrito was always something to look forward to in the morning.

-GARRETT

on the sides and rolled up tight, trapping the fillings inside. They are then wrapped in foil to hold them together. Pressure builds up inside the burrito and when you bite into it, fillings go all down your shirt. Or maybe I have an eating problem. At the very least, I am clearly biased against burritos.

BUT WHICH IS THE BEST????

There have been countless debates online and in taquerias across the country centralizing around the age old question: Breakfast Taco or Breakfast Burrito? The funny thing is that it's always the same complaint lobbed back and forth: Breakfast tacos are too small; Breakfast burritos are too big. I'm convinced now that it's really not a matter of preference based on logic, but a preference determined solely by whether you grew up in Taco Country or Burrito Country. You know by now which country I'm from.

Of course, if you grew up in Burrito Country and love them, who am I to tell you that your love is wrong? It's a free country and if you want to marry Breakfast Burrito, by all means, go ahead. But don't expect to see me after the wedding.

I'll be busy in the catering truck, making out with Breakfast Taco and stealing your booze.

TACO TALK

What do most Mexican-Americans say when you ask to remember their earliest memory about any type of food? Grandma's cooking, of course. It's a refried constant: any culinary remembrance from a Latino will always revolve around a grandmother, and mine is no different...

Whenever she'd come up from Brownsville to stay with us, she'd be up at 5 AM, making huevos rancheros, refried beans, frying the chorizo... Normally she'd have my dad run to HEB to pick up some tortillas–as good as her homemade ones were, it was probably too much to ask her to make those from scratch too that early in the morning. There I was, a chubby four year old, stuffing breakfast tacos into my mouth like they were going out of style... you know, thinking about things like that, that's the only time I can ever get in a mood that's best described as "wistful".

-LOUIS

BREAKFAST TACO HiSTORY

Now that the confusion is cleared up, let's get to the meat of this book: breakfast tacos. To tell the story of the breakfast taco, we need to get into some background information on its predecessor: THE TACO.

Probably everyone knows that tacos came to us from sunny Mexico. And you know that a taco consists of a tortilla—corn or flour—folded over some kind of filling: basically a sandwich. The first tacos were made with corn tortillas, long before the Europeans showed up with wheat. The name "tortilla" was a Spanish application, meaning "little cake". To the Aztecs, tortillas were "tlaxcalli".

Corn tortillas still dominate central and southern Mexico, but wheat flour tortillas are more common in northern Mexico, along the border, and in Tex-Mex cuisine. Corn tortillas are made from masa. Masa (a.k.a. masa preparada or fresh masa) is made from dried corn that's been boiled and treated with a strong alkaline solution of lime (calcium hydroxide, not the citrus fruit) that removes the outer husk. The meaty kernel that remains is then ground between stones to make the dough.

Masa is used to make tortillas, tamales, gorditas, pupusas, huaraches, sopes, and a multitude of other Mexican and Central and South American recipes. Fresh masa can be dehydrated and sold as flour, called masa harina. The word "masa" means "dough" and "harina" means "flour", though this pre-packaged masa flour wasn't available in Texas until the 1980s, which might explain much of the reason why flour tortillas became the default in Tex-Mex cuisine. Guerra says of the introduction of wheat flour to Mexico:

"Corn (or maize) is from the Americas, but wheat is native to the area of modern day Turkey. All tacos were originally made with corn tortillas until the people familiar with wheat flour arrived, some time in the 1500's. Areas in Latin America soon after saw wheat production, which made wheat flour available for the first time in history in the Americas. However, the ones that can be truly credited with developing the flour tortilla are the Middle Eastern immigrants that arrived in Northern Mexico. Pita bread, naan, and other flat breads from the Middle East are the ancestors of the Mexican flour tortilla. The original Mexican breakfast taco would have been made with Native American crops such as beans, tomatoes, chiles and corn flour. Eventually the new ingredients that arrived in the Americas were morphed into dishes that Latin America was familiar with."

Like many foods, it's hard to pinpoint the who, what, and when of breakfast taco origin, but the fact that breakfast tacos come standard on flour tortillas is a strong indicator, proof even, that breakfast tacos originated in northern Mexico or Texas and I realize that's not committing to much in the way of factual statements. Guerra postulates that the breakfast taco "evolved rather than being invented" and I'd agree.

An article from the *Dallas Morning News*, 1933, titled "Happy Dines the Mexican and Well" by Elsa Muñoz describes the exotic foods of Mexico to her curious readers as such:

"Another nice way of eating [tortillas] is to spread them with avocado and roll the tortilla tightly, holding it between the fingers as you eat it, like a cigar! These are called tacos. Cheese, chicken, and frijoles may also be eaten in tacos."

She goes on to say that the dishes "most frequently enjoyed by foreigners" are tamales, enchiladas, chiles rellenos, turkey mole, tripe, fritado de cabrito, frijoles, and sopa. So, take that as you will, but I take it to mean that tacos, for as accessible as they seem to us, were not one of the first Mexican foods to be widely adopted.

A later article from the *Brownsville Herald* dated 1945 introduces the taco as the "Mexican sandwich, or maybe the sandwich is the American taco" and takes pains to describe in great detail:

"The traditional taco has to be fried … [the] tortilla is folded along the middle and fried in lots of hog fat. Ground meat, down Mexico they use shredded meat, is mixed with whatever sauce or garnishment may strike the taco-maker's fancy. A well-made taco is crunchy and delicious."

I found a multitude of articles and menus like these that indicate the growing popularity of Mexican food in Texas from 1930 through the 50s. The 1950s, though, were really

Do Like The Charros--Eat Mexican!

Delicious Foods Can Give Fiesta Real Atmosphere

When celebrating Charro Days, do like the Charros do. And that includes eating what Charros eat. A great many Mexican foods are built around tortilla and chile. Tortilla and chile is so popular in Mexico that there is even a little bird that flies around the flat lands crying, "Tortilla-con-chile! Tortilla-con-chile!"

Of course you know what tortilla taste like, unless you are a "tierno," meaning your green. An American once said that the taste for tortillas has to be acquired, but that once you get to like them you can't leave them. There's something in that dry, limey taste of the tortilla that makes it taste so good, especially with other foods. Used as a combination spoon and fork, it conserves your silver.

Springing directly from the tortilla is the taco. The taco is the Mexican sandwich, or maybe the sandwich is the American taco. Be it as it may, not all tacos are made in the kitchen. Many a taco is made at midnight by the icebox. But the traditional taco has to be fried. It consists of a specially prepared tortilla, made with chile colorado, red chile, and smaller than regulation tortilla. This special tortilla is folded along the middle and fried in lots of hog fat. Ground meat, down Mexico way they used shredded meat, is mixed with whatever sauce or garnishment may strike the taco-makers fancy. Sometimes it's lettuce and tomato, maybe aguacate salad. But don't forget the hot chile, the chile piquin, that small red-like green pepper that burns like heck. A well-made taco is crunchy and delicious.

Enchiladas is another tortilla product. It is called an enchilada because one of its main ingredients is a thick, red chile sauce, something that is "enchilado" —doubt, but the enchilada usually "isn't as hot as other Mexican foods. Besides the red chile sauce and the tortilla, the enchilada is mostly white cottage cheese round into powder. The tortilla, fried pliable this time, is wrapped deftly around the powdered cheese and the red sauce is poured on top.

Then there's tamales, everyone has heard of tamales. They are made of a specially prepared cornmeal dough which is smeared on a piece of cornhusk. Then spiced meat is added and the doughed husk is wrapped tightly and boiled. There are "Turkish" tamales, and also "drunks," the "Turcos" have almonds and raisins. The "drunks" are fat tamales made from the leftovers of a "tamalada". They

CHINA TEXANA—And here is our own variety of the China from Puebla—the China Texana, pictured very appropriately in a setting of Lower Rio Grande Valley Grapefruit.

do not, like other tamales, have the meat-filled center. In the Mexican kitchen, when the meat runs out in a tamalada, they mix what scraps are left with some frijoles and knead this into the dough that has not been made into tamales. Then the fat "drunks" are made from this. They are delicious.

Popular among Americans are "migas" only Americans call them by the tradename of Fritos. When the Mexican housewife finds that her cupboard is almost bare, she will take a few of yesterday's tortillas, soak them in water and cut them into small pieces. These pieces she will fry in fat and add a sauce. Other times she will make "Mexican toast"—what is she will fry whole tortillas in fat to brown crispness. This is what Mexico's cousins know as Fritos.

Tacuaditas are a variety of tacos. Here the tortilla is fried without folding, and the meat and garnishment are placed on top. Each one of them is a miniature plate lunch.

A very popular dish is frijoles. There are several ways of making delicious frijoles One is frijoles refritos, which is frijoles fried, mashed into a pulp and then fried again. They are very tasty and form a good base for several bottles of beer. Some people prefer frijoles caldudos, or soup de frijoles, we could call it. When the beans and boiled, most of the water is left in them, and they are this way and a pungent spices are added. They make a wonderful stew.

Speaking of stews, another wonderful Mexican dish is menudo made from tripe. Menudo provides

the pleasant ending to a night of gayety. Its chief virtue is that it fried this way and pungent spices machs and it is better than tomato juice for making green faces pink.

Cabrito, young kid meat, is a favorite among Mexicans. Cabrito is done in a variety of ways. Cabrito asado—broiled on coals. Cabrito en sangre is made with a sauce of the animal's blood. Cabrito en salsa is made with tomato sauce. The kid's head is often barbe-

cued, and eaten—tongue, brains and all. The eyes are considered an especially delicious tidbit.

Asado is the ancestor of that awful North American dish, Chili Con Carne. Asado, usually made with pork and known as Asado do Puerco, has chile and it has meat, but it is not exactly Chile Con Carne. The meat is diced and fried with a thick red sauce. Different meats are made with mole, especially fowl. Mole is a sort of sauce which is used for

Continued on Page 12

when recipes for huevos rancheros, tacos, guacamole, frijoles and even migas became commonplace in cookbooks, magazines and home kitchens all over Texas.

Fast forward to 1959. An entrepreneur named Joe Acosta began selling bean and egg tacos on "tasty flour tortillas" on the streets of San Antonio. Who knows. He very well may have started the whole thing.

1973 Del Rio, Texas. Del Rio is about 150 miles due west of San Antonio and sits right there on the border, staring Ciudad Acuña in the face.

AP Wirephoto

Restaurant owner Osvaldo Rodrigues ... "Jimmy Carter Taco" a big seller.

The 1970s were a boom year for Mexican food all over the US, and also when we start to see many Texas restaurants offering egg tacos for the morning meal.

And then you know what happened in December, 1976?

Osvaldo Rodriguez of San Antonio, inspired by the election of President Jimmy Carter (the former peanut farmer) started serving peanut and egg tacos at his Mexican restaurant. His customers dubbed it "The Carter" and it became a regular menu item. Fortunately for you and me, the AP article (which was run in at least 6 different papers nationwide from 1976-1977) describes the taco nicely. I've included my recreation of The Carter taco for you in the recipes section.

By 1977, breakfast tacos had fairly fully entrenched themselves into Texas culture. By the 1990s, they'd become so commonplace that practically no restaurant open before 11 am would be caught dead not offering some kind of morning taco. Austin and San Antonio have developed a (somewhat) friendly rivalry over who makes the best breakfast tacos and as much as I hate to admit it, I'll have to agree with Guerra who says, "San Antonio whoops Austin" on breakfast tacos. But ultimately, I'd have to give top prize to the Valley. And it's all thanks to the tortillas. As you move farther south towards Mexico, the flour tortillas get thinner, softer, chewier, and just plain better. Continue to the next chapter to read about how different taco shacks compare from Austin and beyond.

1977 Breakfast Taco Ad.

Seguin, TX.

Menu text visible in image:
- IGAS & EGG
- EAN WITH CHEESE
- EXTRA ITEMS .25
- PICADILLO
- BARBACOA
- PORK IN RED SAUCE
- TINGA DE RES
- CARNE DE RES IN GREEN SAUCE
- BURRITOS, PLATES, NACHOS, GORDITAS

MY BREAKFAST TACO TOUR

In order to illustrate the wide world of breakfast tacos in which each taco has something unique to offer, I decided to do a Taco Tour and chronicle it for you, dear readers. ⫸⟶

We began one Saturday morning at TacoMex, a literal hole in the wall on Manor Road next to the RBM food mart. We tried the chorizo and egg and cactus and egg tacos. Maybe it was just that we were all starving and kind of hung-over but those tacos were really damn good. They were fat little dudes, rolled up in fresh and chewy flour tortillas. The chorizo was

nicely spiced and greasy enough to make a statement but not so greasy that I got orange stains on my pants. The nopalitos were great: big pieces, tangy, and not overcooked. I always forget how much I love nopalitos and eggs: a nice, light follow-up to the chorizo and egg. Their green salsa was avocado-based and spicy and I love it. I could eat it with a spoon until the cows come home and take it away from me because it's so good even cows like it.

Next was **Mi Madre's**, right down the street. It had been several years since I'd been there. (Although the last time did result in a love connection from the front dining room through the glass and into the parking lot, which culminated in a phone conversation in which I deeply offended the singer/songwriter by declining his offer to take a walk in a secluded area.)

The interior has changed a lot, but the people are still super friendly. We tried the migas taco at the proprietor's suggestion and the vegetarian refried bean and cheese taco. The migas won, hands-down. The tomato and onion was just barely cooked, providing a great textural contrast to the scrambled eggs and Colby-Jack cheese. The refried beans were also very good: smooth and creamy like they should be. Did I mention free chips??? Did I mention free awesome chips??? And a nice, fresh-tomatoey, black peppery salsa, too. Thank you for being good to me, Mi Madre's.

Then we got around to Chu-Mikal's on east Seventh Street. I admit, this place does not look like the place to go for amazing breakfast tacos. For one thing, there is a big sign out front advertising a hamburger special. For another, once we got inside, everyone was eating toast or pancakes. But we had a job to do. We decided on a chorizo and egg and a sausage and egg taco. It was a little slow getting them but once we did, I was really glad I had picked the chorizo. I had no problem getting those crispy, spicy chunks of sausage into my face. I guess that's why it took time: crispy sausage bits must be created. The tomato-based salsa was fresh and fruity with a solid after-burn. And if I ever do a Hamburger Tour or a Pancake and Toast Tour, this place will be on that list, too.

»»———→

After that it was **Taqueria Los Jalisciences**. There are several locations. We went to the one on East Highway 290, next to EconoLodge, in the building that is shaped like a flying saucer or a sombrero or a flying saucer that was modeled after a sombrero. We tried chorizo and egg, bacon and egg, and nopalitos and egg. The first thing that was bad-ass was that three different tacos only set me back a cool $2.91. The second thing that was bad-ass was they were piping hot, which means you can leave them in your car for an hour and they will still be plenty hot. Wicked! The tortillas were really fresh and thin, and I would bet they are made with lard like Taco Jesus intended. There was a low egg-to-other-stuff ratio in all of them, which I appreciate. The nopalitos were nice and fresh, the chorizo spicy, the bacon crisp. And three different salsas means three different tastes for every taco bite.

There are a hundred thousand more spots to get great breakfast tacos in Austin. Here's some other favorites:

» Maria's Taco Xpress
» Tamale House (Airport Blvd or East locations)
» El Chilito
» Torchy's Tacos
» Taquería Arandinas

And of course, I'd be doing you a disservice if I didn't include my favorite non-Austin taco spots. These are the places I never miss an opportunity to visit if I'm within 10 miles of them.

San Antonio's **Blanco Cafe**, one of the oldest restaurants in the city, is known for their breakfast tacos. Their flour tortillas are fresh and hot, thicker than some, with a delicate dusting of toasted flour all over. They are sturdy enough to stand up to the sauciest of salsas which is good, because with their green table salsa being as downright delicious as it is, you're gonna want to put a ton on there. On a recent trip, we enjoyed machacado and egg tacos with pico de gallo — ask for it a la Mexicana for more heat — and weenie and egg tacos which are exactly what you're afraid they are. Remarkably, surprisingly good if you like weenies, and I do. One interesting twist: what I call "migas", they call "chilaquiles". More research needs to be done to find out if this is a San Antonio thing or a Blanco Cafe thing. The chilaquiles taco was topped with heaps of grated American cheese, another mark of quality Tex-Mex food. ⫸⟶

In the Rio Grande Valley, **Taco Palenque** is a small Texas chain beloved by locals and for good reason. The flour tortillas here are the kind the Valley is famous for: thin, stretchy, shiny, with nary a trace of any floury residue. The salsa bar at Taco Palenque is truly a sight to behold. Seven salsas made fresh daily, along with icy bins of lime wedges, cilantro, onion, carved radishes, shredded cabbage, roasted jalapeños, pickled onions and more. It's impressive. We tried a bean and cheese taco and a migas plate. The bean and cheese was steaming hot as it should be and went most excellently with some fresh diced onion and red salsa. The migas were made from eggs, corn tortillas, onions and peppers with no tomatoes around. They were damn good covered in melted white cheese and served with papas con chorizo. I went out on a limb and also ordered a beef fajita taco for breakfast, which a couple of old men in Western shirts at a nearby table thought was pretty hilarious, but it was awesome and I'd do it again in a second.

Surprisingly, I'd heard many good things about the breakfast tacos in the convenience stores along the border, specifically the **Stripes** chain. Guerra describes it as "a taco war on the border. Every gas station girds themselves with piles of every type of taco imaginable, hoping to lure in the work crews as a morning muster point." Because there is such a high turnover, the tacos are always fresh and you can get a taco plus a coffee for about a buck and a half. Tough to beat that deal, even if they didn't roll their own tortillas right there in the store, which they do.

PART TWO

HOW TO MAKE BREAKFAST TACOS

TORTILLAS

Tortillas are available at most grocery stores now. So, you know ... thank God, right? Store-bought tortillas are definitely miles ahead of where they were when I was a kid. If you buy them, which is perfectly fine with me, moisten them with a few sprinkles of water or wrap in a damp towel before heating them in the microwave (a few seconds for each tortilla you are warming up) or just toss them on a griddle, or right onto the gas stovetop for a few seconds. This softens them and makes it easier to wrap around your filling and gets rid of any staleness from sitting around on the shelves.

If you want to go all out, making your own flour tortillas isn't hard, but there's a learning curve. I wouldn't count on presenting your first few dozen to El Presidente. This would probably be a fun activity to do with kids, too. I don't allow children in my house, so don't quote me on that, but if you have some kids lying around you might try putting them to work with tortilla-rolling duty. They will probably turn out just fine, and it will leave you more time to lounge around in the bathtub with a bottle of bourbon, a box of bonbons, and the pool boy. That is, until it comes time to cook the tortillas, at which point there should probably be some supervision in the kitchen, but that is what the pool boy is for, right?

FLOUR TORTILLAS

INGREDIENTS

- » 2 cups all-purpose flour, plus about 1/2-3/4 cup more for kneading (you can also use half white and half whole wheat flour)
- » 1 ½ teaspoons baking powder
- » ½ teaspoon salt
- » 2 tablespoons oil
- » 3/4 cup milk, room temperature (water is an acceptable substitute)

INSTRUCTIONS

1. Combine dry ingredients well. Add oil and milk. Mix to form a soft dough. Turn dough lump out onto a floured board and knead for 2 minutes.

2. Add small amounts of the reserved 1/2-3/4 cup of flour as you knead. After about a minute, the dough will change from very soft and squishy and easily torn to firmer and stretchier. At the end of 2 minutes, it will be a smooth ball, no longer sticky, but elastic. The total amount of flour you will need to knead depends on the humidity and other scientific variables.

3. Put this beautiful bouncy dough ball back in the bowl from whence it came and cover it with a damp cloth for 30 minutes. This resting step should not be omitted—it allows the gluten molecules in the flour to relax to make it possible for you to roll them out and also to possibly take over the world.

4. After 30 minutes, come back and divide the dough into 8 to 12 equally-sized balls. Easiest way to do it is to divide in half, then each half again, etc. The balls will be about the size of a golf or ping-pong ball. Put the balls on a plate and let them rest another ten minutes. Patience.

5. Come back and on a lightly floured surface, pat each ball out flat to start it, then with your floured rolling pin, roll into a circle about eight inches in diameter. Remember when rolling stuff out: start at the middle of the circle and push out to the edge. Then back to the middle and towards another edge. Keep going around until you have a circlish thing that looks like a tortilla.

6. Once you've gotten the hang of it, go ahead and turn your cast iron skillet or griddle on high heat. Make sure to use something that can withstand high temperatures (not Teflon). Let it heat up sexy-hot while you continue to roll out tortillas. When it's hot as hell, throw a tortilla on there. Turn the heat down to medium-high. After about a minute, it will start to grow bubble-warts. When those bubbles have almost covered the whole surface of the tortilla, flip it over for another thirty seconds or so. Put it on a plate or keep in a tortilla warmer and do that with the rest of your dough discs.

7. These are best served right away but if you must store them, wrap them tightly in plastic or foil or an old bread bag with a twisty tie from out of the trash bag box, which is what I do since I am "ecological" and also "poor."

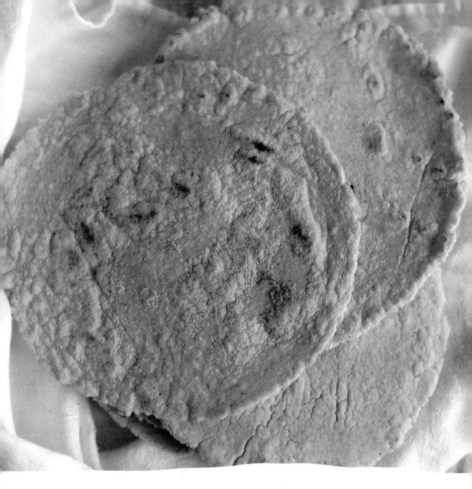

CORN TORTILLAS

Making corn tortillas in many ways is easier than homemade flour tortillas. The original corn tortilla recipe is only two ingredients: masa and salt. Masa harina is dehydrated masa and also called "instant masa mix". Maseca is a very popular brand of masa harina. I use Maseca at home, but if you are lucky enough to find fresh masa, you may use that instead.

These tortillas can be stored for a few hours in the oven if stacked and wrapped in a clean cloth, then either wrapped tightly in foil or placed in a ceramic or otherwise heat-proof tortilla warmer, and placed in a 150-200° F oven. To store leftover tortillas, keep tightly wrapped at room temperature for up to a day, then refrigerated for longer storage. Dampen them slightly with a sprinkle of water from your fingertips before reheating in the oven (wrapped in foil) or microwave (covered in a damp towel) or straight on the griddle.

This recipe make 8 tortillas, but can easily be doubled. A tortilla press is super-duper helpful but not totally necessary. If you don't have one, use a heavy pot lined with plastic to mash them out. Or pat them out by hand.

INGREDIENTS

- » 1 cup (4 ounces by weight) masa harina
- » 2/3 cup warm water (approximate)
- » 1/8 teaspoon salt (optional)

INSTRUCTIONS

1. Line a press with plastic wrap and preheat a dry heavy skillet or comal (griddle) over medium heat.

2. Combine the masa harina and salt in a bowl.

3. Stir in about ½ cup water. Add water in small amounts while mixing with your hands until a soft dough is formed. You should be able to squeeze the dough with your hands to make a ball, but it should not stick to your hands. If it's too dry, add a few drops more water, if too wet (sticky) add a little more dry flour.

4. Roll into 8 golf ball-sized balls.

5. Once skillet is hot enough that a few drops of water sizzle, begin pressing the balls out into tortillas with your plastic-lined press or heavy pot.

6. Cook one or two at a time on the hot skillet, one minute on the first side, then 30-60 seconds longer on the other side.

7. Wrap in a clean cloth to keep warm and absorb condensation while you cook the rest of the tortillas.

SALSA

Salsa is a necessity. It can make or break your taco. A kickass salsa should be spicy, tart, and fresh enough to perk up whatever you're throwing it on.

Although "salsa" just means "sauce" in Spanish, most people in the United States immediately think of salsa roja: the spicy, tomato-based condiment that pals around with baskets of chips on the tables of Mexican restaurants nationwide. It goes by a number of aliases: red sauce, picante sauce, salsa, or just plain hot sauce. It may be cooked or uncooked, mild or hot, chunky or smooth ... there's so many variations, it's mind-boggling.

There are a myriad of other-colored salsas, though. Red is only the tip of the salsa-berg. Here are my favorites.

SALSA DE AGUACATE

"Green sauce" is usually made from tomatillos and peppers. Sometimes—and it's getting more common now—you'll encounter a salsa verde made with avocado. This variation is super delicious, all creamy and just a little spicy. And you'll find my recipe for it below. It is green and good and especially perfect with nopalitos or chorizo tacos.

INGREDIENTS

» 1 avocado
» juice of 1 lime (¼ cup juice)
» ¼ cup water
» ½ cup cilantro leaves
» 1 green onion (cut off roots)
» small garlic clove (½ teaspoon)
» ½ to one whole serrano pepper
» ½ teaspoon salt

INSTRUCTIONS

1. Cut the avocado all the way around long-ways and twist the halves apart. Remove the pit. Scoop the fruit out of the shell and into a blender jar.

2. Coarsely chop the green onion, garlic, and pepper. Whiz everything together in a blender on high speed until smooth.

3. Refrigerate until ready to serve.

4. This keeps for about 48 hours in the refrigerator. Makes about 1½ cups of salsa.

SALSA NEGRA

"Black sauce" is made from roasted tomatoes and peppers or dried chile peppers or both. It has a deep, smoky flavor and is usually pretty spicy so you might want to try before you buy, so to speak. Guajillos are really very mild peppers, so you can probably handle it with the seeds left in. If you want it hotter, you can add a chile de arbol to the guajillos, or add a chipotle pepper for smokiness and hotness.

INGREDIENTS

» 3 guajillo chiles
» 2 Roma tomatoes
» 1 clove garlic
» ¼ cup cilantro leaves
» 1 tablespoon red wine vinegar
» ¼ teaspoon salt

INSTRUCTIONS

1. Toast the chilies over a flame or in a dry skillet. Cover with boiling water and soak for 20 to 30 minutes. When they are softened (they will turn a brighter red color as they soak), pull the stem off and rinse the seeds out if you like.

2. Roast the tomatoes whole under the broiler for about 4-5 minutes per side until soft and blackened.

3. Put everything in a blender along with ¼ cup of the soaking liquid. Whiz it around until smooth.

4. This gets better after a day or two in the ol' fridgerator. Makes about 1 cup.

PICO DE GALLO

"Rooster's beak" is made from diced, raw tomatoes, onion, chilies, cilantro, and lime juice. More akin to a chopped salad than a sauce, it's used like chutneys are used in India. It's heftier than a condiment, but not quite a side dish.

INGREDIENTS

- » 1 cup diced tomato
- » ½ cup diced onion
- » ½ cup minced cilantro
- » 1-2 jalapenos, diced or minced
- » 2 tablespoons lime juice
- » ½ teaspoon salt
- » ½ teaspoon minced garlic, optional

INSTRUCTIONS

1. Combine and refrigerate thirty minutes to blend flavors.
2. Keeps refrigerated 48 hours. After that it gets less appealing. Makes about 2 cups.

SALSA ROJA

INGREDIENTS

- » 5 Roma tomatoes – seeded (blanch and peel them if you want to, but this is supposed to be easy)
- » ¼ cup chopped onion
- » 1 clove garlic, mashed
- » 1-2 jalapenos (cut out membranes and seeds for less hotness)
- » 2-4 tablespoons lime juice (start with two and add more if you want after tasting)
- » ½ teaspoon salt
- » ¼ cup cilantro

INSTRUCTIONS

1. Combine tomatoes, onion, garlic, jalapeno, lime juice, and salt in a blender. Whirl it around until it is smooth. Taste to adjust for lime juice and salt. Mix in cilantro.

2. Set aside for an hour in the icebox to let the flavors blend. Makes about 2 cups.

THE
CLASSICS

Now that you have a stack of homemade tortillas at the ready and a bowl of salsa chillin' in the fridge, it's time to get the guts made.

As determined earlier, the protein part of the guts is what distinguishes a breakfast taco from a "taco for breakfast". You have two options: eggs or beans, refried I hope. Eggs are more common, but beans are perfectly acceptable and delicious to boot.

Once you've got your protein, there are three more standard options that every self-respecting taco stand or restaurant will offer: potatoes, bacon, and pork breakfast sausage. And there you have the Five Musketeers of breakfast tacos. (Cheese, avocado, and salsa are just the sidekicks.)

Of course most restaurants offer more than five filling options and depending on the kind of joint it is, they vary from chorizo to nopalitos to calabacitas (summer squash) to Mexican rice to machacado; I'll call those the Five Other Dudes, just to make it official. So pick two or three out of the Five Musketeers or one of the Other Dudes, put them in a tortilla, add some cheese and salsa, sit back, and enjoy, knowing the love of a good taco is right there with you. Keeping you strong. Loving you from the inside out.

SCRAMBLED EGGS

I'm sure you know how to make scrambled eggs, but in the interest of comprehensiveness, here goes anyway. Only tip I'll offer is this: one egg per taco is a little bit too much when you've got multiple fillings on offer. The ratio I suggest is 3 eggs:4 tacos. For example, if you're serving a crowd and want to provide the makings for 12 tacos, use 9 eggs to avoid having a bunch of leftover and potentially wasted scrambled eggs.

INGREDIENTS (FOR 4 TACOS)

- » 3 eggs
- » 1 tablespoon butter
- » ¼ teaspoon salt
- » ¼ teaspoon pepper

INSTRUCTIONS

1. Beat the hell out of the eggs. Use a whisk if you have one. And you need not bother with adding water or milk. Just seriously whip those eggs. You want to get some air in there. If you're making a whole lotta eggs, you can even use your blender! Add salt and pepper.

2. Heat a heavy-bottomed 8 or 10 inch skillet over medium heat. Use a larger one for more eggs, but remember a thicker layer of eggs is easier to control (i.e. not overcook) than a thin layer. Melt the butter in it. You can also use a nonstick skillet with some spray oil if you must, I am not trying to kill you. »———→

3. Let the butter get foamy. Pour in your eggs and leave them alone about 30 seconds. Stir gently with a wooden or silicone spoon. Stir frequently while they cook for small soft curds; stir less frequently for larger curds of egg. Cook over a medium-low heat and take them off the heat before they are completely dry — they should still look glossy and shiny but firm. There will be enough residual heat in them that they will finish cooking on your plate in your taco.

EGGS IN THE MICROWAVE

This is possible and very helpful when, as it happens, every surface of the stove is covered in bubbling pots and whatnot. It's very easy to overcook eggs in the microwave, though, so follow these instructions and heed my advice, child. Primarily, don't try to cook more than 6 eggs at a time in the microwave.

INGREDIENTS

» 3 eggs
» 1 teaspoon butter or some nonstick spray
» ¼ teaspoon salt
» ¼ teaspoon pepper

INSTRUCTIONS

1. Get a microwave-safe bowl and spray the inside with oil or smear with the butter. Crack the eggs into the bowl and whisk. Add salt and pepper.

2. Cover with a microwave-safe plate or lid and microwave 30 seconds. Remove (it might be very hot!) and stir. Cover and cook another 30 seconds. They might be done by now. If not, stir and cover again and go another 20-30 seconds.

REFRIED BEANS

INGREDIENTS (FOR 4 TACOS)

- » 2 tablespoons vegetable oil or lard
- » 1 clove garlic, minced
- » 2 cups cooked pinto or black beans*
- » water (or liquid from cooking the beans)
- » salt

INSTRUCTIONS

1. Saute the garlic in the oil or lard for a few seconds over medium-low heat.

2. Add some of the beans and mash them up. A potato masher works, but so does a big spoon. Add some more beans, mashing after each installment. Add about ¼ cup of water or bean-cooking liquid if they seem dry.

3. Keep stirring and mashing, adding more liquid if necessary, until you have a big, steaming skillet of fairly smooth, well-fried beans. It should be about the consistency of mashed potatoes or a little thinner. Add salt if it needs it and some oregano if you're feeling it.

*TO COOK BEANS FROM SCRATCH:

1. Sort the beans. Take heed: I too was once of the mind that sorting was unneeded until the woeful day when I chomped into my chalupa and bit on a rock. Put one pound of dry beans in a colander and *really* look at them. Pull out any funky beans or anything that is not, in fact, a bean. Then rinse them and put them in a big ass pot.

2. Cover them with 6 cups of water and throw in 2 or 3 big cloves of garlic—peeled and smashed open. You can also chopped onion, oregano, epazote and/or a bay leaf.

3. Put a lid on it and bring it to a boil over high heat. Stir it around and turn the heat to medium. Cover again and cook at a solid simmer for 1 hour and 15 minutes. Check them. They should be tender throughout, but not yet falling apart on their own accord.

4. When they are perfect, you can pinch one (caution: hot!) with your fingertips and squish it open easily. It might take 2 or 3 hours to cook if the beans are older. Add probably 2 teaspoons of salt now and taste the broth to adjust the seasoning. Makes 6 cups cooked beans.

HOME FRIES

The key is using cold, cooked potatoes for extra crispiness. Leftover baked or boiled potatoes work perfectly. Skin on or off.

INGREDIENTS (FOR 4 TACOS)

- » 1 cup cooked, diced potatoes
- » 2 teaspoons canola oil or lard
- » ½ teaspoon salt and pepper
- » ¼ cup diced onions (optional)

INSTRUCTIONS

1. Heat a heavy cast iron skillet on high for one minute. Add your oil. It should immediately turn hyper-fluid and start moving and shimmering all over that skillet. Swirl the skillet around to get the oil everywhere.

2. Add your potatoes in one layer. Leave them alone for a minute. Shake the pan. They should be moving freely. Leave them alone again. Shake the pan every minute or so to make sure they aren't sticking.

3. When they're good and brown on the bottom, stir them around to get the other sides brown. Shake the pan some more. They will probably take about 8 minutes total. If you want onions, add them in after about five minutes. Just keep shaking, flipping, and browning until they are toasty as a pair of kittycat mittens. Salt and pepper those puppies and you got it made in the shade.

BACON

TO COOK BACON ON THE STOVE

You probably know this, but I'll go over it again anyway in case you don't.

1. Start the bacon in a cold skillet, arranged in a single layer. Turn it to medium heat and cook, turning a few times, for 10 to 15 minutes. Thick-cut bacon takes longer.

2. Drain on a paper towel or a brown bag or some newspaper like we did in the old country. If you need to keep it warm, transfer to a baking sheet and hold in a 200°F oven until needed.

TO COOK BACON IN THE OVEN

This is my preferred method when cooking large amounts of bacon, such as when entertaining large crowds of hungry people, and extremely convenient when you have the stove already covered in skillets of eggs, potatoes, tortillas, and beans and who left that margarita machine on the counter?!

1. Get a baking sheet and put some kind of rack on it, the biggest you have, the kind for cooling cookies works well.

2. Lay out bacon in a single layer, trying not to let the sides touch too much. Bake in a 350°F oven for 20-30 minutes. Don't need to flip or anything. Easy Peasy.

TO MICROWAVE BACON

If you've never microwaved bacon, it might scare you. I was scared, thinking it was going to light my microwave aflame. Plus, it sounds possibly gross. But it's not. It's actually a really satisfactory way to make crispy bacon and Here's how to do it:

1. On a microwave safe plate put down 2 layers of paper towels. Lay out your bacon, not overlapping or touching.

2. Cover them with another paper towel. (Yes, it's a HUGE waste of paper towels and I don't like it any more than you do but microwaved bacon is still a good trick to have in your back pocket.)

3. Microwave on high for 2 to 3 minutes, depending on how much bacon you're cooking, then check it.

4. Rearrange the strips, moving the center pieces to the outside and vice-versa. Be careful, the bacon and the plate is real hot. You may need to change the towels if they are soaked. Keep going, checking every 30-60 seconds until it's done to your liking. Voila.

HOMEMADE
CHORIZO

Mexican chorizo is a fresh sausage that must be cooked before ingestion unlike Spanish chorizo, which is cured. They are not interchangeable. Though easy to find, many brands are overly greasy and made with "less desirable" cuts of meat (yet still delicious). Chorizo is also easy to make at home.

If you make it yourself, you can make it lighter by using a lean cut of pork. (I suppose you could also make it heavier by adding ground pork rinds or straight-up lard but I don't think that would help matters.) Or maybe you live in a forlorn place where you can't buy Mexican chorizo. Then you have no choice!

Either way, when you make those chorizo and egg tacos for your friends, it's fun to be able to say, "I made that! I am super awesome and the best cook EVER in the whole universe!!!"

INGREDIENTS

- » 1 pound finely ground pork
- » 2 ancho chiles
- » 1 large garlic clove
- » 2 tablespoons cider vinegar
- » 1/4 teaspoon each of ground coriander and cumin
- » 1/2 teaspoon dried oregano
- » 1 teaspoon salt
- » 1 tablespoon paprika
- » 1/16 teaspoon (a pinch) allspice

1. Toast chiles in a dry skillet or over the gas burner of your stove. Don't burn them, please. Just a few seconds will do. Place them in a bowl and cover them with a cup of hot water. Let them soak at least 30 minutes.

2. Remove and discard the stems (and seeds if you want to decrease the heat). Put the peppers in a blender with the garlic, vinegar, and ¼ cup of the soaking water. Blend to a fine paste.

3. Combine pork, chile paste, and all other spices in a mixing bowl. Mix with a paddle attachment, a big spoon, or by super-duper clean hands. Refrigerate, covered, 24 hours. This is not required, but it makes a better tasting sausage.

4. To cook chorizo or regular breakfast sausage, heat a skillet over medium-high heat. Crumble your sausage into it. Stir it around, breaking up big chunks into smaller chunks and getting it nice and brown and crispy. When it's done, it should be brown everywhere and not pink anywhere.

You can drain some of the grease off now, but why?

HANGOVER TACOS

I wanted to mention this video because it's my favorite taco to have after a long night at home of drinking, dancing, drugs, and passing out in the yard. Chorizo and eggs will heal your broken head and belly. In the video I demonstrate how to cook more than one taco filling in the same skillet so that each sleepover guest with juggalo makeup on his face can customize his taco with his preferred ratio of ingredients.

hilahcooking.com/hangover-tacos/

NOPALITOS

Nopales are cactus pads; nopalitos ("little nopales") are cut-up cactus pads. They have a similar texture to okra—tender-crisp and kind of...wet—while they taste like... sour. But, green? It's hard to explain. But, they are a high fiber, low calorie, refreshing way to fill up your tortilla and worth a try if you haven't had them before.

Both are commonly found fresh in grocery stores in Texas, but maybe not so much elsewhere. If you can't find fresh nopales, check out the "ethnic" food aisle at your store for jarred nopalitos. They are fine and easy. Here's how to prepare either:

JARRED NOPALITOS: Rinse well and drain in a colander. The purpose is to get off the brine in which they are packed because it's probably very, very salty. Heat a skillet over high heat; add a teaspoon of oil and a chopped green onion and your drained nopalitos. After about 5 minutes when they are good and hot with a little toastiness, they are ready. You can add some beaten eggs at this point if you like. Cotija cheese goes especially well on top.

FRESH NOPALES: If present, cut out the spines carefully, wearing heavy gloves and using pliers and a paring knife. If you managed to get your paws on some fresh, spineless nopales then you get to skip this step and more power to ya.

Slice them lengthwise into ¼ inch strips and then into 1 inch sections. Heat a tablespoon of oil over high heat. Add a chopped green onion and the nopalitos. Lightly salt them. They will turn a slightly darker green and let off some slime as they cook. As they cook further, the slime will mostly go away. Cook, stirring, for 10 to 15 minutes until they are tender, a bit browned, and nearly slime-free. Now you can add beaten eggs if that's your plan.

TACOS
ESPECIALES

THE CARTER

Based on the "Carter Taco" introduced in 1976 by Osvaldo
Rodriguez, this taco combines two cheap proteins: eggs and
peanuts. It sounds weird and it is, kind of. I found that with
the addition of fresh sliced jalapeños and onions, though,
it becomes a lively little taco reminiscent of pad thai. Top it
with some chili-based red salsa to add heat.

INGREDIENTS (FOR TWO TACOS)

- » 2 eggs
- » 3 tablespoons roasted peanuts
- » 2 teaspoons butter or peanut oil
- » 2 flour tortillas, warmed
- » fresh jalapeños, onions, cilantro or pico de gallo

INSTRUCTIONS

1. Beat the eggs well. Season with a little salt if your
   peanuts are unsalted.

2. Chop the peanuts to about the size of a match-head.

3. Melt the butter in a small skillet over medium-high heat
   and add the peanuts. Cook, stirring, until toasty (about
   60 seconds).

4. Add the eggs and reduce heat to low. Stir until the eggs
   are cooked to your liking.

5. Serve in warm flour tortillas with condiments of your
   choosing.

MIGAS

INGREDIENTS (FOR 4 TACOS)

- » 2 tablespoons oil
- » 3 corn tortillas
- » 6 eggs
- » 1/2 teaspoon each of salt and pepper
- » 1/3 cup chopped onion
- » 1/3 cup chopped, seeded tomato
- » 2 tablespoons minced jalapeno
- » 1/4 cup grated cheese
- » 1/4 cup chopped cilantro
- » 4 flour tortillas, warm

INSTRUCTIONS

1. Heat up your oil in a heavy skillet over medium-high. Slice your tortillas into ¼ by 1 inch strips.

2. Fry those little boogers for a few minutes until they get crispy and browned. Remove from the skillet and set aside.

3. Saute the vegetables, except cilantro, in the remaining oil for a couple minutes until softened. Reduce the heat to medium-low

4. Add your eggs (which you have beaten the hell out of and salted and peppered like I showed you in the scrambled eggs video) and half the tortilla strips.

5. Sprinkle them with cheese and continue to cook.

6. Add cilantro and the rest of the tortillas when the eggs are almost ready. Ta-Da! Migas! Now make a taco. Eat it.

You're welcome.

GREEN EGGS & HAM TACOS

This is a cute and delicious way to figure more green leafies into your diet. If you can't find chilaca peppers, use half of a poblano. They have a similar flavor and heat. Also try using crispy bacon in place of the ham. A bright, limey salsa verde works well with these.

INGREDIENTS (FOR 4 TACOS)

- » 4 eggs (or 2 eggs plus 4 egg whites for a greener taco and less fat/calories)
- » 1 chile chilaca
- » 1 clove garlic
- » 2 green onions
- » 1 cup arugula or spinach
- » ¼ teaspoon salt
- » 2 teaspoons butter
- » 4 slices Canadian bacon or ham, halved
- » 4 tortillas, warm

INSTRUCTIONS

1. Beat eggs thoroughly in a bowl.

2. Combine coarsely chopped chile, garlic, onions in a food processor and pulse until chopped. Add arugula or spinach and salt and pulse a few more times until all are finely chopped.

3. Heat butter in a medium skillet over medium heat and saute vegetables for about a minute until slightly softened. Add eggs and mix together, cooking until beginning to set.

4. Move eggs to one side and heat bacon or ham briefly.

5. Assemble tacos with "green eggs" and ham!

SWEET POTATO & BLACK BEAN

A delicious vegan option, this taco was inspired by the sweet potato and egg breakfast taco from Austin food truck, The Peached Tortilla. It was then further inspired by a breakfast taco I got from Cherrywood Coffeehouse in Austin with my own combo of beans, mushrooms, and potatoes and to my surprised delight, the potatoes were shoestring cut and deep fried to make lovely, crisp and light potato croutons on my taco. For my version here, I've used fried shoestring sweet potatoes on creamy refried black beans. For a lower fat version, saute the potatoes in just a tablespoon of oil until crisped. Top with something vibrant and tart like salsa verde or pico de gallo and add avocado for some healthy fat.

INGREDIENTS (FOR 4 TACOS)

- » 1 medium sweet potato (about 9 ounces weight)
- » 1 ½ to 2 cups refried beans (black beans are nice, but pinto are good, too!)
- » 1 cup peanut oil or your preferred oil for deep frying
- » Avocado slices, salsa, pico de gallo, cilantro, lime wedges for serving
- » 4 corn or flour tortillas

INSTRUCTIONS

1. Peel the sweet potato (optional) and slice thinly (I used a mandoline to get 1mm slices) stack several thin slices together and cut into 1mm strips with a sharp knife.

2. Heat oil to 350ºF in a deep pot.

3. Add half of the potatoes to the oil. It will sizzle and bubble up for about 30 seconds, then relax. Give them another 30 seconds or so and remove with a slotted spoon or spider to a plate lined with paper towel to drain. Fry all potatoes this way.

4. Spread warm tortillas with a couple spoonfuls of warm beans, top with crispy potatoes and any salsa or additional ingredients you like.

The best I ever had was about ten years ago in Brownsville, Texas. It was a Mexican place, I can't remember the name of it for the life of me, but it was in a strip mall that had the breakfast taco equivalent of a make-your-own-omelette bar. And for only $1.50 a taco. And I had like ten bucks on me. You picked all the fillings you wanted, they cooked it up for you behind a sneeze-guard, you stand there, arms quivering in anticipation, waiting for the illegal chef to slide it off onto your waiting plate. I had four tacos, all with the same idea: as much Mexi-meats as possible. Each taco was loaded up with a mixture of barbacoa, chorizo, migas, bacon, potatoes and comically generous scoops of pico de gallo, all colliding and colluding on a tiny stack of corn tortillas. And, because I need a nourishing liquid to wash it down, a Fanta. That's like orange juice for fat people, right?

-LOUIS

LOU-CHADORE: MEATY PARADISE

I had to take some liberties here, since the average Joe might find it difficult to buy barbacoa. I'm sure Louis won't mind.

INGREDIENTS (FOR 4 TACOS)

- » ½ pound Mexican chorizo
- » 2 hot dogs
- » 2 eggs, beaten
- » ¼ cup grated Cheddar or American cheese
- » 4 flour tortillas
- » Pickled jalapeños
- » Pico de Gallo

INSTRUCTIONS

1. In a large skillet, fry chorizo, breaking up with a spatula into small bits, until fully cooked and crispy.
2. Thinly slice the hot dogs and add them to the skillet, getting them a little crispy in the chorizo grease.
3. Pull all the meat aside and add the eggs. Stir gently until almost set.
4. Divide eggs and meat between tortillas, add cheese.
5. Top with pickled jalapeños and a comically large scoop of pico de gallo.

My mom and her side of the family is from New Mexico, the land of green chile. If I am going to make breakfast tacos at home, I always try to throw in some roasted green chiles. Many times, the breakfast burritos in New Mexico are smothered in the spicy sauce. If you happen to visit the Land of Enchantment, be sure to ask for the green chile on the side until you know whether you like the taste and can handle the heat!

-GARRETT

THE HEATH: AN ENCHANTING GREEN TACO

I doubled down on the green chili for this one.

INGREDIENTS (FOR 4 TACOS)

- » 1 tablespoon vegetable oil or bacon fat
- » 1 cup diced potato
- » ½ cup diced onion
- » 1 - 4 ounce can diced green chiles
- » ¼ teaspoon salt
- » 3 eggs, beaten
- » 1 tablespoon butter
- » ½ cup green salsa
- » 4 flour tortillas

INSTRUCTIONS

1. Heat the oil over medium-high heat and fry the potatoes and onions for several minutes until soft and brown. Add the chiles and salt and heat through.

2. Cook the eggs separately in the butter until just set.

3. Divide eggs and potatoes between tortillas and top with green salsa

Thanks for Reading!

I hope this book has inspired you to make and eat as many break-fast tacos as you can during your short life. We only have, like, two more years until the glaciers are melted and the ocean overflows and sharks come knocking at the door, so let's make them count, people. On the up-side, ancient pirate booty will probably come floating right up to your window, too, so at least you'll be rich, even if a shark ate your foot.

A round of applause for my interviewees. Check out their websites for recipes and restaurant reviews:

Addie Broyles

theFeministKitchen.com

Louis Fowler

twitter.com/LouisFowler

http://www.okgazette.com/

Melissa Guerra

MelissaGuerra.com

Garrett Heath

SAFlavor.com

Hilah

Made in the USA
San Bernardino, CA
04 March 2014